Jawahir Altamimi is a young poet who found herself between letters, words and blank pages. Writing is her way to talk and speak to those who have watered every single feeling inside her. In her opinion, she thinks that a pen can do more than a million speaking mouths.

I dedicate this book to all the neglected souls that didn't find their place in this world. These pages are here to engulf you through your bittersweet phases.

Jawahir Altamimi

FIRE THROUGH ASHES

AUSTIN MACAULEY PUBLISHERS™

LONDON • CAMBRIDGE • NEW YORK • SHARJAH

ISBN – 9789948778127 – (Paperback)
ISBN – 9789948778134 – (E-Book)

Application Number: MC-10-01-9080214
Age Classification: E

Printer Name: iPrint Global Ltd
Printer Address: Witchford, England

First Published 2024
AUSTIN MACAULEY PUBLISHERS FZE
Sharjah Publishing City
P.O Box [519201]
Sharjah, UAE
www.austinmacauley.ae
+971 655 95 202

I would like to present my gratitude to whoever supported me through this journey. It was such an honor to carry your support between my fingertips.

Sometimes we misunderstand our self-worth and we start questioning people around us about where we belong. We belong to ourselves and to the people we deserve. Get up every day out of your bed and clean the old dust on your chest, light a fire out of your ashes and forget about your regrets.

As the sun shines, and the rays hide beneath my skin
I remember you like it was yesterday
But when I notice my heart and the way it beats
I know that you are gone and nothing's left to feel pleased
How unfair and wise to still remember you
Even on my worst days
Like the sun, you shine everyday
But isn't it a misery that I could never reach you one day?

Sometimes we are tired of all the places that we called home
Sometimes we carry a world of pain in our bones.
Sometimes we are stuck with hearts made of stones.

When your absence starts hitting me
When the miseries find a place in me
Don't come back and throw your false apology in my face
Just pray that somewhere else I will be free.

I hope you learn how to say sorry meaningfully.

I stood by the window, waiting for the magic
The magic was you…
And that was simply tragic.

I wonder if sometimes you ask yourself if I still remember
you
I wonder if you want to crawl to me just to ask me how did I
forget you
If I'm being honest
To forget you, I stayed away from all the places
All the places that are filled with memories with you
To forget you, I stopped meeting the people that knew about
you
Just to avoid their questions about how it is going between
me and you
To forget you, I built a strong relationship with insomnia
Just to avoid dreaming about you
To forget you
Just to forget you.

An ocean can't fall in love with a lake.

Sometimes I am red because of the blues.
But sometimes, I start to think that I was born blue and with
time I turned purple.
But now, I have decided to mix green with my redness and
dress my soul up with a colorful yellow.

You were a museum filled with art
The art of love and the art of lying
They both found a place in you.

From time to time, you will feel like the universe is reviving the sad love in each day.

I dreamt of you again
I was still in love with you like my reality
And you were over us continually
I had a dream about you
I woke up feeling blue because here is not where I belong
I'd rather sleep forever if that's the only way I can be with
you
In my dreams, my only dream
My only dream.

I saw the lies inside your eyes
Through your voice and your sweaty hands
I saw the lies and I swept aside my hunch.
I saw the lies and chose to stay quiet.

I spent nights and more nights missing you
And that was little hurtful.
But I spent seconds, minutes and many hours
Denying it
And it felt more like agony.

It's all about the memories.

Honey,
I feel you
everywhere
Even in my bones
I feel you
Even when you are elsewhere.

Don't lie don't lie don't lie don't lie
Don't lie don't lie don't lie don't lie
Don't lie don't lie don't lie don't lie
Don't lie don't lie don't lie don't lie
Don't lie don't lie don't lie don't lie
Don't lie don't lie don't lie don't lie
Don't lie don't lie don't lie don't lie
Don't lie don't lie don't lie don't lie
Don't lie don't lie don't lie don't lie
Don't lie don't lie don't lie don't lie
Don't lie don't lie don't lie don't lie
Don't lie don't lie don't lie don't lie
Don't lie don't lie don't lie don't lie
Don't lie don't lie don't lie don't lie
Don't lie don't lie don't lie don't lie
Don't lie don't lie don't lie don't lie
Don't lie don't lie don't lie don't lie
Don't lie don't lie don't lie don't lie
Don't lie don't lie don't lie don't lie
Don't lie don't lie don't lie don't lie
Don't lie don't lie don't lie don't lie
Don't lie don't lie don't lie don't lie

Please do not lie.

Sometimes I sleep to meet your shadow
Sometimes I sleep and in my dreams, I wallow.

Do you understand how it feels to crawl on your knees and beg God to turn off the fire that has been set in your heart?

There was a time when you asked me to stop loving you the
way I do
That time I swallowed all the love I still have for you
And I whispered to you,
"My love is strong. I can still love you in any way you want
me to."
I stayed
I stayed for the sake of the person that I thought I knew
But now, I'm talking to someone new
And I still can't believe this is the same person who once
made me bloom
Sometimes, I wish I chose to leave
At least I could've kept your memory sweeter than you
could ever believe
Sometimes, I wish I chose to leave
Before living in grief
I wish I chose to leave.

And I can barely remember
The way you used to call my name.

Love,
I had my mind set on leaving
But you…
How can I leave you?
But also, how can I keep you?
I'm not confused
I know that my heart wants you
But I also know it doesn't need you.
I know that my brain hates you
But my veins still pump you.
And while you were getting cursed by my brain
My heart called you by your name
And it all went blurry
All over again.

All I asked for was hearing your voice once again.

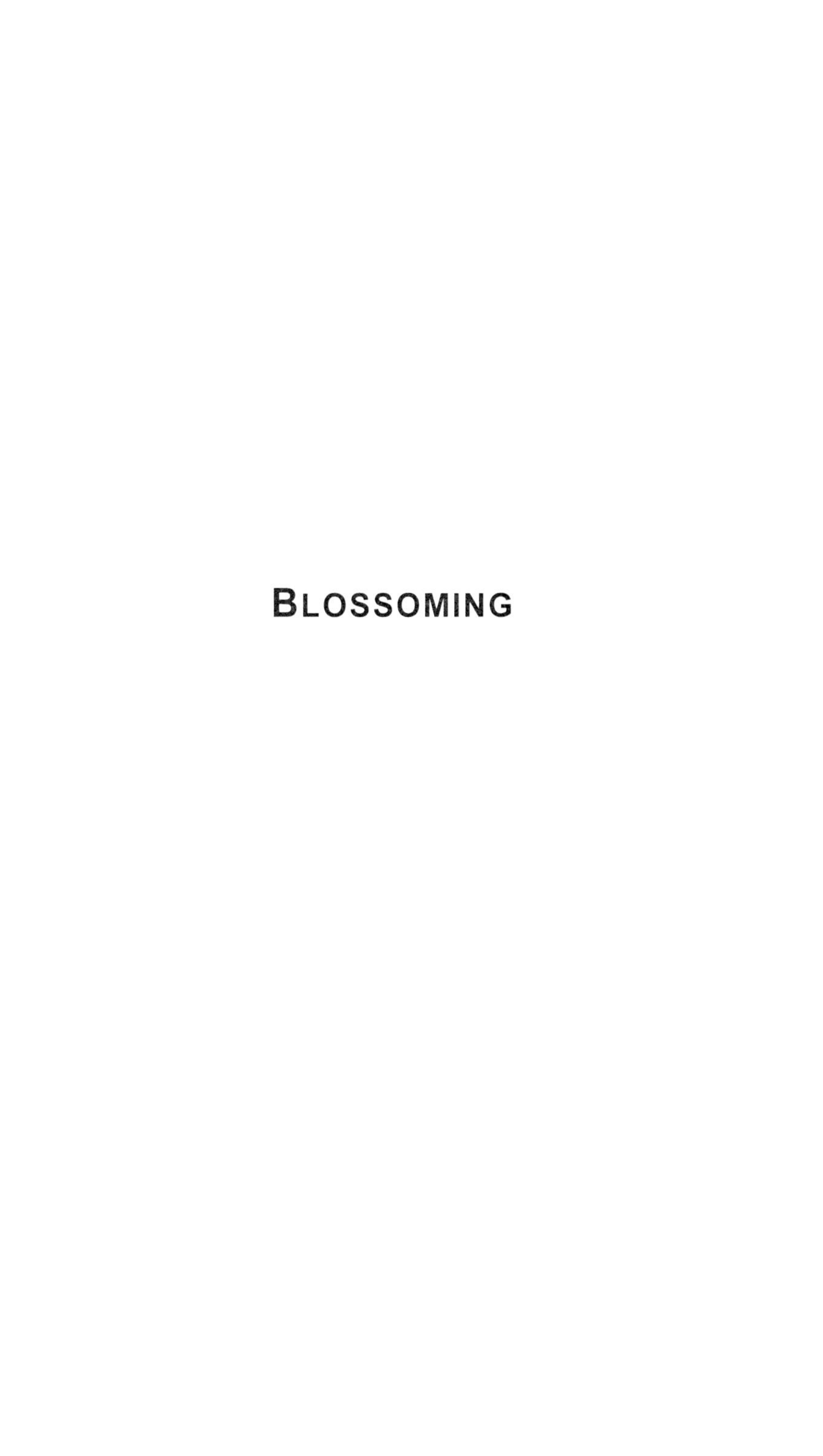

BLOSSOMING

I was crumbling last night
And those tears of mine
Felt like raindrops
And it made me realize
There is good in every bad
Even when it gets tough.

Being mad at the world will not change it.

Sometimes,
There's love in hiding your love.

Darling,
I won't allow you to break me
Or allow me, myself, and I to shed a tear over you
I'm not who I used to be
I'm not the cloud who used to weep
I'm the sun
I get up everyday
To rise and breathe.

I've always wanted to offer you love
Even in the middle of your ongoing wars.

Changing and maturing are two different things.

I kept my heart closed after you.
And unfortunately, that's what kept the pain
Now that my heart is open again
All the aches found an exit
And my own worth started to regain.

Today, you might wake up with a heavy heart
But tomorrow make sure to clean the old dust that dwelt in
your heart
Tomorrow, healing will come to us
It's not too far.

I had to deal with it alone
Alone.
Alone.
Alone.

Stop saying I might
I believe it's time for you
To say
I will.
You will.

With time, you will learn how to disentangle your tongue to
face the anger that found a home underneath your ribs
Maybe you will ease the heaviness in your heart
Maybe, hopefully you will see things differently and begin
with a new start.

Today,
I still remember you,
But with less water in my eyes.

Sometime toxicity can't be treated
Leave
Leave
Leave
Leave
Leave
Leave
Leave
Leave
Leave

You should know,
I can still write with a closed wound.

I love myself
Beyond your imagination
I love myself
Note that if you tried to bruise my soul
You are not welcomed in my world anymore.
I worked hard to bring my soul back to light.

What's better than hearing your mother's voice through the walls, asking God to protect your heart?

I still get up every morning
To sit on my sofa with a cup of my darkest coffee
As the sun shines on my ribs
I stare into my papers
They are white, just like my dress
I take a deep breath
And start uncovering myself
On these empty papers
Oh, what a bliss
These empty papers
What a bless.

I'm writing what I'm feeling.
You are reading what you are feeling.
We can feel each other.

To love yourself is the beginning of yourself
To love yourself is to be honest with yourself
To love yourself is to accept yourself
Love yourself,
Gleefully and Shamelessly

Little sweet girl,

You have every right to talk about your dreams repetitively.
Your dreams.
Your.
Dreams.

Sometimes, we wonder if we are going to get through the
darkest days.
Sometimes, we wonder if we are going to stay happy like we
are today.
We are fashioned by God in this way,
To go down and ignite ourselves to the brightest flame.

If one day you caught yourself
Questioning your worth
Trying harder to keep the bonds
Making excuses when deep down you know it's wrong
Being cruel to yourself
Being cruel to yourself
Building mountains of anger on your backbone
Waging wars on something inside you that is unknown
Run.
Run, sweetheart.
Run as far as you could.
Run, it was all misunderstood.

Depression and all the delusional thoughts it causes.

I don't look for love in others,
I offer/give it to myself.

I loved you but I love myself more and that made you burn,
please bear in mind that nothing could ever make me desert

myself.

Myself.

Myself.

Myself.

It's been a while
But I still try
To take you out of my broken spine
It's been a long time
And your shadow won't stop passing by
And that scent of yours still makes me cry
It's been a while
But I still want to try.

They say, "blood is blood,"
Trust me, blood was still blood when you chose to betray
me.

The moon,
I pledge my life to the moon.

The stars,
They speak to me.

The beach,
A healer.

I love it when it rains.

I don't need to cry you a river to show my empathy
I don't need to scream and weep to show you that something
is hurting me
Sometimes I laugh when I'm sad
Sometimes I laugh when I'm happy
Last time I laughed when my heart got heavy
That time they thought I was acting unmannerly
I laugh
When I'm sad
I laugh when I'm happy
I laugh when I'm hurt
I laugh when I'm shocked
I laugh
Through tears and blood
I laugh
When I'm sad and when I'm happy.

11 RULES

Rule number one: don't re-read the old messages.

Rule number two: don't re-read the old messages.

Rule number three: don't re-read the old messages.

Rule number four: set your mind on wanting to leave.

Rule number five: don't wait for them to look for you when you disappear.

Rule number six: don't talk about it or you will feel everything all over again.

Rule number seven: don't look back or you will be lost.

Rule number eight: mend your broken pieces on your own.

Rule number nine: don't look for a healer.

Rule number ten: keep in mind that your heart is broken but it isn't gone.

Rule number eleven: go to the beach.

Read it all over again.

And when I decide to talk
I rush to the rooftop
Where I sit there facing the moon
To talk
To laugh
To grief
To blast
The moon
Bright, quiet, and beautiful
The moon
Bright.
Quiet.
Beautiful.

FOR US

FOR THE SAKE OF
ALL BODIES

It took me some time to start talking about my own body,
but now that I have started writing, I realized that it does not
matter how I'm going to start.
I surely know that I was born with the body I have, the body
I own.
But what you don't know is that I braved thousand storms to
have the acceptance that I have now for these magical parts.
And with time,
I learned how to love my body respectfully.
Respectfully.
Respect.
Fully.

My dear,
We owe our body an apology for not loving it
wholeheartedly.

Beloved,
In every storm we will face thunders, and it is ok for our bodies to keep a good memory of this thunder beneath our skin.
-stretch marks-

FEARSOME ROAR

74

I'm a summer storm
Do not underestimate the things
I'm willing to do

REMINDER,

Our height is just a number. Our weight is just a number.
Our skin color is a gift,
A gift from God.
From dark to light
And
From light to dark.
Still a gift from God.
From God.

The thing about us is that sometimes we tempt to search for happiness in other souls.
The thing about us is that we expect acceptance in the wrong spots.

Do not wait for them to offer their acceptance.

It only takes you one step to be successful
1- Believe in it

I am who I am
With no fear and without an apology.

Give yourself time to grieve
Not a short time
Not a long time
For time is running
And life is fleeting
Give yourself time to grief
But give yourself a chance
Your mistakes will not be the last
For we are humans
We go wrong
But we can still go right.

Not every flower belongs to your garden.

Some flowers want from us to dig deeper
And gardening is not my thing.

Live in your present

Live in your present

Live in your present

Live in your present

Live in your present

Live in your present

STRETCH MARKS

It's artistry
It's a memory
It's a tale
It's a story of change
It's who we are
It's us.

Dear mother,
I know how many times you have burned your soft hands
I know it hurts you, but you'd always smile and ask us,
"How is the food?"
Mother, I love you.

Miracles exist
In you

WOMEN,

You are **charming**

You are **heroine**

You are **whole**

You are **empowered**

You are **inspiring**

You are **confident**

I'm who I'm
I accept myself
I love myself
I'm worthy
I'm lovely
I deserve to be happy.

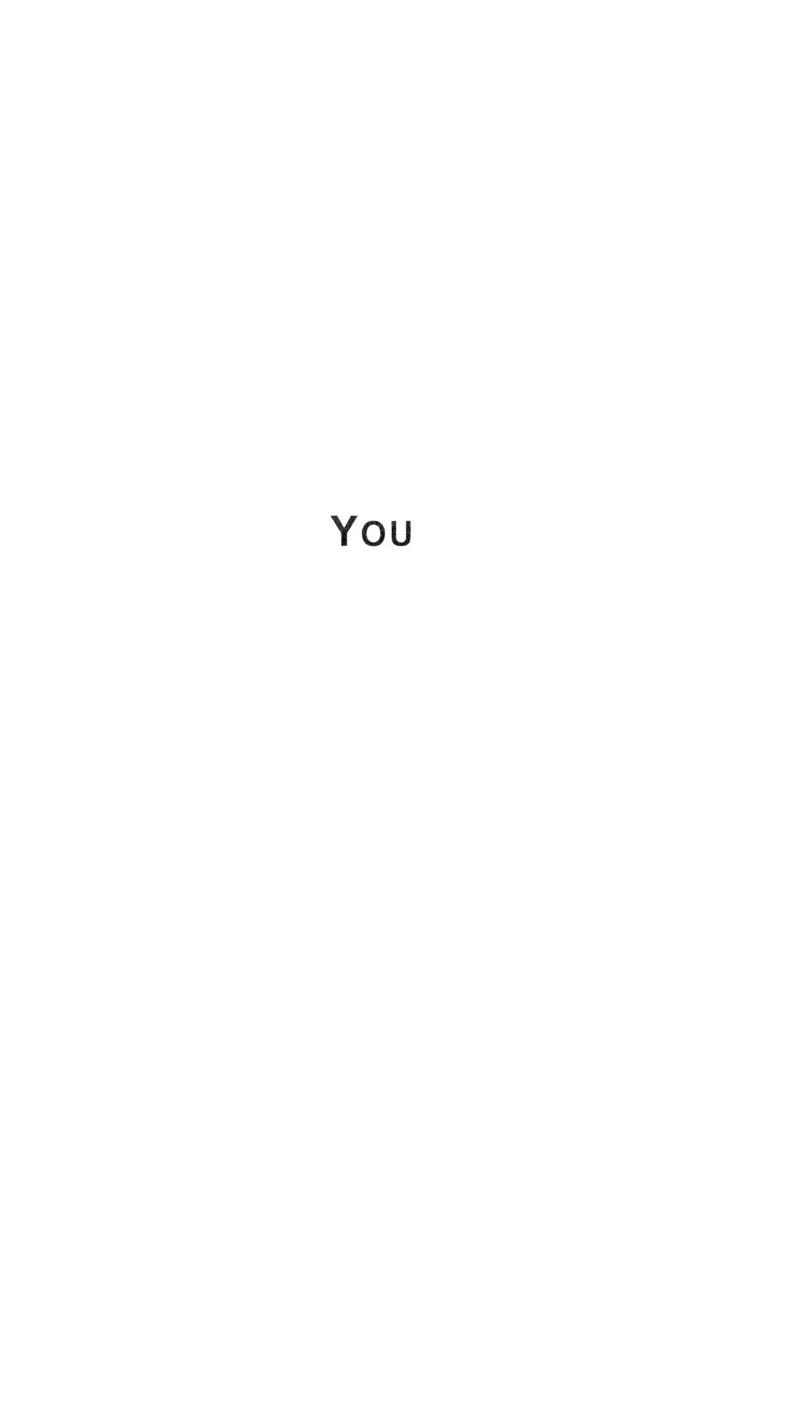
You

You,
You have softened me.

If tomorrow comes and I was unable to talk about how I feel
I think it's more than fair to start to believe
That words are not always the key
I know I did not speak
But look, I'm still here
I knew you are different to me
When I started to think about you
Since I wake up until I fall asleep
When your shadows started visiting me
In my reality and in my dreams
But you will know your are different someday
When I choose to hold you when the world starts to shake.

Honey,
You brought me a double walled cup
And I still refuse to drink my coffee in another mug.

For our first of everything
I'm still thankful
For our peaks and valleys
For the laughter and tears
For the love
For you
For us
I'm thankful
Always thankful.

You felt like home
My only home

Honey,
I can write a thousand books
To explain what I'm hardly trying to say
But not a single page
Will ever be enough for me at the end of the day.
Look into my eyes
And read the words you are craving
Although I poured my heart out on these pages
And my feelings ended up getting their wages.
Look into my eyes and leave the book
For they are waiting for your eyes to look.

Rain heals and the wind is anger released.
But all the universe's rain could never wash the memories
out of my brain.
And all the world's wind could never turn off my heart's
flame.

I wrote and wrote and wrote
And I wrote a little more
And added some more
But you know
And I know
Words never say it all.
For it can't lift all the heaviness
Only the heart knows
And all the poems in this world
Could never describe this chaos.
Only the heart knows
And not a single feeling of mine
Was explained well in these words.

I'm the warmth in your bed when you wake up.
I'm the fire in your heart when you get up.
I'm the pain in your throat when you speak up.
I'm the candle who used to light you up.
I'm the good in your bad.
The good.
In your bad.

I filled this book with thousand words
But this page is different
This page is specifically for you
And only you
Read it until you understand
Every word and what it means.
If I gave you my book
And you wondered why
It is because many unspoken words
Were spoken in letters
And many hidden thoughts
Were frozen within the book's feathers
If I gave you this book
I hope we get the chance to read it
Together.

143

Dear NK,
Thank you friend
For all the love you give.
And all the joy you bring.
Thank you for every second we spent.
Thank you, my friend.

Dear S, H,
We are family,
Even if it's not by blood.
We are family,
By heart.
Thank you.

Dear SZ,
You saved me many times,
Thank you.

Dear RA,
You give abundantly,
Thank you.